NO MORE KICK-CAN AND COBBLES

NO MORE KICK-CANS AND COBBLES

by
Michael John Fowler

Wharncliffe Publishing Limited

First Published in 1997 by
Wharncliffe Publishing
an imprint of
Pen & Sword Books Limited,
47 Church Street, Barnsley,
South Yorkshire. S70 2AS

*For up-to-date information on other titles produced under the
Wharncliffe imprint, please telephone or write to:*

**Wharncliffe Publishing Limited
FREEPOST
47 Church Street
Barnsley
South Yorkshire S70 2BR
Telephone (24 hours): 01226 - 734555**

ISBN: 1-871647-42-8

A CIP catalogue record of this book is available from the
British Library

Printed in Great Britain by Redwood Books, Trowbridge,
Wiltshire

Contents

*This book is dedicated with
love to Liz, Chris and Kyle and in memory of
Glynis, a wonderful sister, who was very much
a part of my early years.*

And so out went the carefree swinging 1960's and in came a new decade of the 1970's; with a greater growing awareness for me. Hippies and flower power disappeared, and in place there emerged a more yobbish culture of Mods and Rockers, Skinheads and Greasers; whose violent clashes leapt from our monochrome televisions.

It was a time of not only noticeable local change within my environment, but national change, as pounds shillings and pence gave way to decimalization. Joining the Common Market was only a vote away; though not for me.

As the decade began the Mexborough I had known at a tender age was being modernized. My old 'stomping ground' of cobbled alleyways and back-to-back housing were being demolished, as the local council felt it necessary for the town to develop.

Ancient landmarks had to make way for more modern buildings and amenities, and in some areas whole neighbourhoods were uprooted and relocated as a new bypass was built to allow faster links with neighbouring towns.

In my own home the tin bath became redundant, save for washing the dog, as Council grants allowed us the installation of a full bathroom suite. For the first time hot water came straight out of a tap. For me the modern era had arrived.

This nostalgic collection of stories and photographs follows the successful 'Legacy of our Backings' and depicts the changing face of Mexborough that I remember as a juvenile. It is the final chapter in my celebration of all those times we so fondly call 'the good old days'.

Hopefully it will stir vivid memories of your own past, wherever you lived.

Michael John Fowler

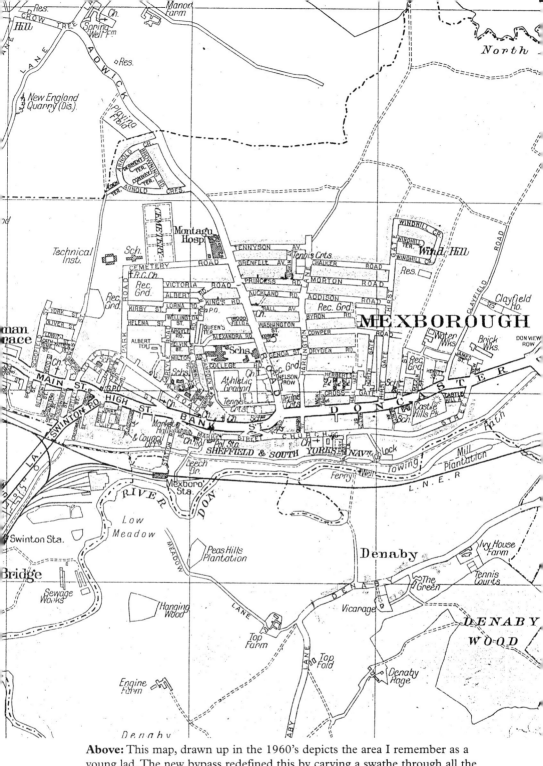

Above: This map, drawn up in the 1960's depicts the area I remember as a young lad. The new bypass redefined this by carving a swathe through all the streets just below High Street and Bank Street. It took away Cresswell Street, Cliffe Street, Glasshouse Lane; dissected Station Road and continued its demolition process into Oxford Road, Market Street and finally Pinfold Lane.

Above: This more detailed plan show the location of the streets which I so fondly refer to as my 'stomping ground.' Some of these roads and housing disappeared in the late 1960's and early 70's

Above: High Street, facing in the general direction of Bank Street. Shop blinds, such as shown above, are very rare today. Shops and buildings to the right have been demolished for a new precinct and the road has become pedestrianised.

THE SPIRIT OF CHRISTMAS PAST

'This is just what that theer famous actor wears, thar knows,' said Martin, as he rubbed a dollop of brown make-up on my face. 'Laurence Olivier – thar knows; him who did that Shakespeare Play – Dick the Shit.'

I frowned. 'Dick the Shit?'

'Dun't crease thee face it'll leave white lines.' He began to chuckle. 'Yeah – Richard the Turd.' The chuckle became a guffaw and I found myself giggling with him.

'Shurrup blaspheming in't church.' I felt hot breath on my neck as a gruff voice hissed above.

Michael was a lot older and a far more serious Thespian in the Nativity play. 'Thy'll get struck down by lightning,' he finished, pointing up to the beamed roof space, as he pushed his arm through the hole in a blue velvet curtain, which had been

Below: High Street, facing in the general direction of Bank Street. All the shops on the right have now gone.

altered, replicating something reminiscent of a King's robe.

The only reason I had got involved in the Nativity play, at St. George's church, on Main Street, in the first place, was because I had been persuaded to join the choir. The only reason I had joined the choir was because it promised funds of one penny (1d) for attending practice and threepence (3d) for Sundays and weddings. It was an additional source of money towards the fortune I dreamed of.

'Rub it in all ovver thee mug and when thar puts thee 'eadband on, thar'll look like a real shepherd.' Martin was still rummaging through the box of brightly coloured blankets, old curtains sewn together and hessian sacking, that would costume us into an overall biblical effect for the play.

Michael thrust a fluffy wollen toy lamb into my arms. 'And cuddle that 'til it's thy turn to see babby Jesus, then thar leans it against his crib. Mek it stand up so it dun't look like it's dead.'

He placed a fez on his head and I smiled. 'Thar looks like Tommy Cooper.'

His face creased into a grimace. 'Look this is serious. Me Mam and Dad are gonna be out theer tonight to see us perform, so dun't prat about. Does thar understand?'

I glanced across at Martin who displayed a sort of 'who-does-he-think-he-is' type of look.

'And thy ain't got any words to say, so just act natural,' he finished.

It was all right for him to say that. There would be pews and pews of people for this once in a year event, and I was a bag of nerves.

Within half an hour, as we put the final touches to our costume, hushed voices had increased to an abundance of natterings outside our changing rooms, as the church began to fill; and the butterflies, within my stomach, were fluttering wildly.

The evening drew on swiftly. We performed well in front of the audience and at its conclusion we even raised a hearty applause.

However unforeseen to anyone mortal, disaster loomed on the horizon as we travelled back in a troupe, down the aisle.

It actually commenced when the lamb slipped from my grasp and I tried to scoop it back up without anyone noticing. Unfortunately the Shepherd behind hadn't seen my predicament and was still clomping forwards, concentrating on the words of 'Once in Royal David's City' which flowed sweetly from his lips. He hit my arched back in full stride. I shot forwards, stumbling onto the swirling robes worn by Michael, garbed as the Frankincense King, and because his head was poking only through a mere slit, cut into the centre of the altered velvet curtain, it yanked his head backwards, whipping sharply into his Adam's apple, converting his voice from Soprano to Baritone in mid-song. His fez shot off at an angle and his gold box clattered to the floor.

As laughter reigned around, Michael's eyes bore down with such livid hatred in them, that I felt it necessary to blame the lad behind. So much so that when we finally composed ourselves and speeded up towards the sanctuary of the changing room, Michael shook the living daylights out of the Shepherd, as I gave my finest performance as the innocent party.

Below: Even this more up-to-date photograph, taken in the late 1970's, has changed today. The road no longer exists, instead a modern brick and paving pedestrianized precinct is in place, and many of the shops and stores have changed hands and had their frontages updated.

Above and below: Two views of the High Street, both facing in the general direction of Bank Street.

'Crikey it's a bit parky Dulcie.'

I recognized the lady, who stopped us shopping in our tracks; just outside Woolworth's, though I couldn't remember her name.

'Eee ain't your Michael shot up?' I cringed as she patted the top of my head, as though I was a puppy dog.

I appreciated the halt though because it actually allowed me time to scrutinize the new boxes of Betta-Bilda sets, that were displayed inside the shop window, bathed in the store's yellow lights, giving an illusion of warmth.

The window squeaked as I rubbed away the moisture which had accumulated, enabling me to gain a better view of the new Action Man at the back. I marvelled at the latest model which had real hair, moveable eyes and hinged joints.

My balaclava, was suddenly itching my ears and I rubbed at the sides with my mittened hands. The more I scratched the itchier they became, until suddenly my ears were getting hot.

Then one of them became further heated as a clip from Mum

Below: This photograph taken in 1967 shows the demolition of the White Rose Café on Garden Street, to make way for an extension to the Yorkshire Bank. The cafe stood where the bulldozer is parked.

halted my actions abruptly.

'Stop it Michael.'

I recoiled as she scowled down at me before returning to her conversation. 'Anyone would think he had lice.'

The lady shuffled a fraction away from me, just a jerky movement but I quickly registered it from the corner of my eye. I smiled. That'll stop her patting my head, I thought.

'Dun't kids show you up?' Mum added.

The lady nodded and they continued with their women's business.

I loved this time of year even though the weather was cold and almost changed by the hour; from bright winter light to thick black overhead clouds. The shops, at times, were nothing but silhouettes, in the gaunt light, yet the warm glow which emanated from each window, gave off a wonderful and magic aura about the High Street.

I was growing up fast and the 1970's were looming. I no longer believed in Santa Claus, the Tooth Fairy or Easter Bunny. In fact when I was first told Father Christmas didn't exist, I burst into tears. It was contrary to everything I believed and I did initially fear if I accepted this suggestion I wouldn't receive any presents. However I need not have feared, for even with the seeds of doubt swiftly planted in my mind, I still received my gifts on the 25th, finally dispelling the myth of Santa Claus. In the later months my parents finally confessed all.

In spite of learning this latest fact, in yet another maturing aspect of life, I still appreciated all the joy and wonderment of Yuletide; feeling the parcels gingerly, whilst guessing at its shape, before opening.

I had even found the 'secret' place where the gifts were hidden, it was quite accidental. Playing hide and seek one day, I climbed onto the tallboy in Mum and Dad's bedroom and then scuttled on top of the wardrobe, which had been placed at an angle against two adjoining walls. There in the triangle, formed by the corner section, was everything, concealed beneath an old sheet.

Sadly I was too late, they were already wrapped and disguised.

Above: This photograph is of the rear courtyard of Sarah Street. This was a box section of two rows of houses with a cobbled courtyard and several sets of shared outside toilets. This view is facing towards the top set of houses that bordered onto Garden Street. These were demolished in the late 1960's and the cleared area remains as a car park at the rear of the post office.

Christmas was the one time I really felt spoilt. I never really had a lot of anything, so what I did receive on this joyous occasion, became very precious indeed.

The weeks leading up to Christmas were very active. Decorations were home-made and meant gluing together endless reams of coloured paper chains, as well as making delicately cut Chinese lanterns to festoon the downstairs rooms.

With the big day finally looming Christmas Eve was almost as hectic. Early morning shopping for fresh crisp vegetables and a selected turkey, with Mum always complaining about prices being deliberately inflated.

Then it was back home to a roaring fire, with logs hissing and spitting in the grate. Television was filled with a marvellous variety of monochrome adventures which captured my attention, whilst the aroma of freshly baked mincepies wafted from the kitchen.

The afternoon hours were filled with Mum, my sister and I cleaning and polishing and 'hoovering' the house from top to bottom until it gleamed spick-and-span. It was back to the black and white 'goggle-box' as Dad called it, to finish off a busy day.

Below: High Street, looking in the direction of Main Street. This immediate location had always experienced heavy congestion even though it was controlled by traffic lights. Any vehicle parked near here would cause chaos for the buses, who's terminus was just to the left, on West Street.

Above: Swinton Road, looking down towards the South Yorkshire Hotel pub, all the shops prior to McDonalds Bicycle shop have now been demolished. The site is presently used as a car park for Somerfields supermarket.

Below: This photograph shows the terminus on Adwick Road, at its junction with Princess Road.

As 10 o'clock loomed, pillow-cases were fastened to the end of our beds and we were securely tucked up. Sleep took an eternity to come, and when it did it seemed merely seconds before our eyes flicked open. In the darkness my sight adjusted to the surroundings as I probed for the full sack only a few feet away.

As I began to rummage, the rustling noise became overwhelming, no matter how careful I was.

Dad's voice suddenly boomed from the next room. 'Go back to sleep. It's not time yet.'

Don't be stupid I thought. Of course it is. The presents are here. 'What time is it?' I rasped back.

'Half past four. Now go back to sleep for an hour.'

That was an even more stupid thing to say and I sat bolt upright with an opened book I'd managed to unwrap, struggling desperately just to look at the pictures, never mind read the text.

Below: Scenes involving Mexborough's 'trackies'. This one is looking from Swinton Road towards Post Office square.

SPY OUT IN THE COLD

'Now I can wipe out Thrush,' I sneered in my harshest tones as I burst from the yard shed.

'Pardon Michael?' Mum's head spun round, peg poised in mid-motion, ready to clip onto her washing.

It was the manner in which she questioned my comment that halted me in my tracks. 'I can wipe out Thrush,' I repeated, tapping my black Man From UNCLE attaché case.

I had received this as a birthday present. It was a marvellous gift. When opened its interior revealed a metal Luger with silencer and an attachment that transformed these components into a full-length sniper rifle. An innocuous looking packet of cigarettes concealed a small firing pistol, a camera which squirted water and a hidden camera fastened to the plastic sides, which could be operated from outside the case completed its secretive constituents.

The Man From UNCLE held a special place in my heart. Even more exciting than Batman and Dr Who. It introduced me to the world of espionage and spy gadgets that I desperately tried to recreate, as my imagination escaped into the weekly thrilling adventures.

'What do you mean Michael?' She hadn't moved; the washing was still pressed against the line.

'THRUSH Mam.' – I looked at her confused – 'The sworn enemy of Napoleon Solo and Illya Kuryakin,' I said quite indignantly, as though she should know.

'Oh I thought you were on about something else.'

'Something else?' I enquired, what on earth was she on about?

'Never mind, you just get on and play.'

How can anyone understand the mind of a mother I thought as I left my supreme headquarters, which was cunningly disguised as our yard wooden shed.

Paul wasn't in, Robert was going out for the day, Tony and Graham were incarcerated in their rooms for the day, under punishment for fighting. This resulted in me not being able to find a partner anywhere nearby to go out on a spying mission.

NAPOLEON SOLO,
ILLYA KURYAKIN AND
ALEXANDER WAVERLY
KEEP THE WORLD SAFE
FROM THRUSH

U.N.C.L.E.

Above: Plotting the next
UNCLE mission in the
confines of our garden shed.

Dragging my feet along Catherine Street, it was time to venture further afield, to find another associate who wanted to join me as an UNCLE agent.

For a second I could have sworn that the grey-haired man driving the Hillman Hunter on West Road, was an arch-rival of UNCLE. I tried my best not to look like a spy as I aimed my black briefcase, with its concealed camera, in the speeding car's direction. I clicked the trigger inside the handle and another pretend photograph was obtained for my portfolio of enemy agents. It would have been very difficult for anyone to guess my true identity as my triangle I.D. badge was pinned beneath my shirt collar, and the UNCLE emblem on the front of the briefcase was turned inwards against my hip.

On Oliver Street I took out the fountain pen which turned upside down into a pretend communication transmitter. I knocked on Tony's back door and he appeared within seconds, face unusually solemn.

'Hey-op. Are thar coming out?' I tapped my attaché case. 'I thought we'd play Man From UNCLE,' I whispered.

'I can't. I got in late last neet and me Mam says I can't come out.'

'Go on ask her again. I'll let thee be Napoleon Solo. Thar can hold me briefcase.'

His eyelids raised. Turning his head, owl-like, he shouted back inside the house, 'Mam Mick's called for me; can I go out and play?'

'Tony you know what was said, don't you?' His mother's voice drifted from somewhere inside.

He shrugged his shoulder towards me.

'Go on ask her again,' I said, still in soft tones.

'Please Mam, just for an hour.'

'Tony – NO, you can go out tomorrow tell him, but today you stay in.'

As I drifted back down his alleyway I recall thinking that Mr. Waverley never had problems getting his agents to go out on missions because of their mothers.

Above: The weekly adventures of Batman and Robin was another of my favourite shows. I regularly emulated the heroics of these Super-heroes. I even believed that these two could bat-rope up the sheer face of buildings. The Batman suit became a much sought after article yet with its light blue body suit it wasn't exactly a replica. Though at the time I never really realized. And what about that snake-belt!

ONE OF LIFE'S VICTIMS?

'Me Uncle Gordon med it me,' I announced with a degree of exuberance, holding my wooden Excalibur aloft, waving it several times in the air before returning it to its magical sheath; currently disguised as a snake belt. 'He med me shield as well. Does thar like it?' I thrust the plywood knight's protective guard, with its painted red cross, towards Tony's face.

'Gis a go wie it,' he requested excitedly.

'I can't. Me Mam telled me ar want to let it go out of me hands.'

His face gave off a sudden mournful display.

'But I'll tell thee what, I'll ask me Uncle to mek thee one shall I?'

'Will thar?'

'Course ar will, then we can be like them Knights of the Round Table.'

'Yeah,' he gushed.

I began to slap my thigh, holding out a pair of mythical reins. 'Come on I'm gonna Betty's for some bits.'

With a throaty 'neigh' Tony whacked the top of his leg and bolted quickly in front of me, galloping along Schofield Street to Betty Brown's Fish shop, at the corner of Flowitt Street.

In less than two minutes we were demonstrating, in mid air, the art of fastening one's trusty steed to the iron fall pipe outside this shop. The warm and aromatic fatty smell of freshly fried fish and chips wafted into our faces, tickling our nostrils and releasing our gastronomic juices, as we strode into the leaf green interior of Betty Brown's.

Betty's usual bouffant of jet black hair was mostly hidden beneath a crisp white turban style hat, its fringe just peeking out in a Superman style twirl. She glanced quickly up, scrunching together a pair of equally dark eyebrows, and then banged dripping grease from her metal scoop as she slung a fresh batch of cooked chips to the back of the frying range.

'As thar got any fish bits Betty?' I asked watching a pall of steam rise to the cream coloured ceiling.

'I have Michael.'

Betty had known me a good number of years since she had acquired these premises as a sweet shop prior to its conversion as her fish and chip emporium.

I tucked the wooden shield beneath my armpit and leaned forward on the range. Instantaneously I jumped backwards as the searing heat, from the shiny aluminium cover, penetrated into my hands. The shield clattered to the floor echoing round the tiled walls and I blew into now red palms. 'Flippin' eck Betty that's hot.'

'It's supposed to be,' she replied, her richly made up face scowling in my direction and pointing with the silver coloured chip shovel to a small hand-written notice, fastened half-way up one green tiled wall. I could just make out 'Please don't lean on fryer – boiling hot.'

'You need a magnifying glass to read that. It should be pinned on this counter,' I exclaimed still rubbing my hands.

'No it shouldn't, and don't be so cheeky or I won't give you any bits.'

'Can I have a big bag? Me mate Tony'll share 'em wie me.'

'You cheeky little monkey, you're getting these for nowt as it is. You're supposed to buy a bagfull.'

'I wor gonna buy some chips Betty, but me Mam says me Dad dun't get paid 'till tonight.' I pulled out two off-white linen pockets from my grey trousers allowing old pieces of fluff to fall onto the linoleum floor. 'See I ain't got a skerrit Betty.'

She smiled, handing over the bag of fish bits, whilst she scooped another portion of chips out of the bubbling frying fat, to throw to the back of the range.

I handled them awkwardly, having retrieved my shield and tucked it back under my armpit.

'Is there any salt and vinegar for these?'

Her face creased, changing quickly into a frown. 'Take your hook, you little bugger.'

I started to laugh. 'I'm only kidding Betty.' I turned, fish bits in hand, shield gripped tightly against my ribs. 'Hey you're moving to Australia soon aren't you Betty?'

'I am that love – when this is all sold up – no more foggy

mornings for me and three foot of snow. It's sunshine, glorious sunshine nearly every day.'

'My Uncle Brian and Auntie Brenda went to live in Autralia.'

'Did they love?'

'Yep, and my mate Paul Neal's gone there as well. Will you say hello to them when you see 'em?'

Betty fastened her hands onto her matronly hips. 'Michael do you realize Australia is sixty-four times bigger than England? I'll probably never see them.'

'Okay' I shrugged disconsolately. I only asked her to say hello to my relatives and friend I thought to myself, I didn't need a flaming geography lesson.

As I stepped out onto the street the fat from the fish bits was gradually seeping through the greaseproof paper, making my hands slippy and sticky, and I juggled with the bag from one hand to the other.

'Hey-op. What's thar doing?' A voice screamed across in our direction.

When we looked up Derek, who was now skipping towards us, was just opening a newly purchased packed of Champions TV series cards.

'We've just cadged some fish bits. Does thar want some?' I asked proffering forwards the now see-through bag. It was really a ruse, to enable me to spy what cards Derek had got. My own set was almost finished with only a few required to complete the giant picture, on the back, that you had to jigsaw together.

I pushed the bag even closer to his face as I scanned the assortment of cards he had opened.

'Hey I ain't got that one.' I stabbed at a picture of the gorgeous Alexandre Bastedo. 'I'll swap thee.'

'No, I ain't got it mesen.'

'Go on, I need that to nearly finish my set. I'll gie thee five for one, that's a fair swap.'

He paused before answering; prodded around in my greasy bag and picked up several fish bits, which he dropped into his mouth.

'It's a good deal Derek. Ain't it Tony?' I glanced towards my mate hoping for willing support. He nodded in acknowledge-

ment. 'See, Tony thinks so,' I continued, looking square in Derek's eyes.

He finished chomping the bits of crunchy batter, then shook his head decisively. 'No I might not get it again, but if I do you can have first grab.'

My face dropped.

'What's tha playing at anyway?'

'We've been playing knights. Like Ivanhoe thar knows,' answered Tony.

'Can ar play?' Derek folded the pink chewing gum, from the Champions cards packet and slung it into his mouth, then rolled his jaws in an exaggerated fashion.

'If thar swaps me that card thar can,' I replied.

'Gerroff!'

'Well thar can't play then.'

'Gis a go on thee sword and shield.' Derek leaned forward and snatched at my shield. I pulled back quickly, dropping the remainder of the fish bits.

'Look what thar's med me do now, stupid idiot. Betty'll not gie me any more now thar knows.'

'I only wanted to have a go wie thee sword and shield. Dun't be spiteful.'

'Swap me thee card and ar will.'

'Get lost.' Derek made another lunge for the shield.

I pulled it swiftly from beneath my arm, stepped back and held it forwards. Derek made another futile effort in an attempt to grasp it. I leapt to one side, pulling the wooden sword out of my snake belt. Derek didn't know who he was fooling with. As a fully fledged knight I was a man unaffected by nerves having already that day faced the noise of imaginary battle. Taut-faced I skipped skillfully backwards and forwards with competitive ease. Derek made pawing attempts to grab each item, his face colouring in frustration.

'Gis a go or I'll smack thee,' he suddenly snapped.

'Oh aye, thee and whose army?' I proudly delivered in challenge.

'Ar dun't need no army, tha'll see.' He made two or three more half-hearted attempts to snatch the wooden weapons before I'd had enough, and delivered the consequential counter-punch. The speed with which I threw my wooden shield forwards mercilessly exploited Derek's ponderousness. What I had not realized, as it smacked against his head, was that when it had earlier clattered to the floor, in Betty's chip shop, it had dislodged one handle, exposing the sharp end of a fastening nail. Derek's sudden scream was my realization of this.

Blood began to trickle from a nasty nick just above his temple and I felt a wave of nausea surge over me, as I saw what had happened. I shot quickening glances between Derek's bloody head and the destructive nail.

He dabbed awkwardly with his hand at the painful region, and as he pulled back his red palm, he began a fearful wail. 'Thar's had it now Fowler. I'm gonna get thee done now.'

Before I had time to apologize Derek was scuttling hell-for-leather in the direction of his home.

Tony's jaw had dropped. 'Mick what did thar do that for? Thar gonna cop for it now.' He paused. 'Thar'll tell me Mam that I had nowt to do wie it, won't thar?'

Images of the local Constable dragging me away in handcuffs clouded my mind and the pit of my stomach churned as I sloped towards home. I had been so proud of my wooden sword and shield earlier that morning. How could I have realized they would play a part in an untimely downfall. My unkindly act had been pure misfortune. Would I be able to convince others. 'God what happens if I go to prison?' I thought. I shuddered as I scurried towards Schofield Street school, thinking about going into hiding, just like the Fugitive on television.

★ ★ ★ ★

I knew there was trouble by the tone of Mum's voice as she greeted me. 'GET IN THIS HOUSE, THIS MINUTE.'

She was wiping her hands on the flowered pinafore smock that covered her dress. I side-stepped her, never taking my eyes off those rotating hands.

'What have you been up to this afternoon?' The voice was only a mite pitched higher than normal.

'It was an accident Mum, honest,' I exhaled, my mind was functioning on auto-pilot, thinking about the recriminations, whilst answering as best defensively as any loquacious lawyer to exculpate oneself.

'Accident – I'LL GIVE YOU BLOODY ACCIDENT.' The pitch was getting higher. The hands now wiping furiously. 'I've had Derek's Mum here for the past half hour. She's had to have him at hospital all afternoon. She says you've belted him with the sword and shield and split his head open.'

'It was only my shield Mum, and it was only a nick. She's exaggerating.'

'That may be so, but you've used a weapon on him. What have we said about fighting –' her voice trailed off, yet still at fever pitch.

'I wasn't fighting Mum, honest. It was Derek. He was trying to nick my shield, so I pushed him away with it. I din't know it was bust. A nail was sticking out and it caught him on the head. It was his fault – it was an accident.' I was thinking hard now, reminiscing about other things that had happened, when I'd been criticized and blamed, and it hadn't really been my fault.

Take for instance that time, they went mad because I'd let all the rabbits out of their hutches, at the back of Dr Bhatias' surgery on Roman Terrace. Mrs Bhatia was ranting and raving, chasing round, frightening all the bucks and does. That was the reason I'd let them out in the first place because they looked frightened in those cramped cages. They wouldn't let me explain properly for that and I got the blame. There was also the time I saw Mrs Bhatia cleaning her car. I only picked up the hosepipe to help her swill it down. How was I to realize she hadn't wound up the window on the driver's side. It was her fault the interior got soaked, not mine, yet who was it who got blamed for that as well – ME. Or what about the time I was playing cricket in the back yard with a long piece of wood for a bat and the metal ash-bucket as a wicket. It wasn't my fault that I couldn't handle Uncle Gordon's bowling. He should have thrown under-arm not over-arm. Every time I swung at the ball it just ricocheted off the bat's edge. I hadn't entirely been at fault when three of the kitchen window panes got broken.

'I always get blamed,' I suddenly blurted. 'It was an accident.'

'Well I'll show you an accident young man.' Mum suddenly snatched my shield and wooden sword from my grasp. The swift movement also caused me to jump backwards, as much by surprise, as well as terror. 'THIS IS AN ACCIDENT.' She banged the sword over her knee twice, on the second attempt it snapped. She then propped the shield against the back door jamb, smashing down her foot and splintering it with a sharp crack. 'THAT'S AN ACCIDENT AS WELL.'

I'd failed miserably to exonerate myself and the tears welled in my eyes. I hoped she'd hurt her foot doing that. 'It's not fair,' I sobbed 'I always get blamed for everything.'

Above: This view shows the backs of several rows of houses on Garden Street, just before Belle Vue Road. These were demolished in the early 1960's and the area is still waste ground. The little girl at the front of this picture is only known as Valerie. Shortly after this photo was taken, she was out with her mother, a vehicle mounted the kerb, dragged her under its wheels and she was killed.

McDONALD'S
OF MEXBOROUGH

For

AUSTIN and RILEY CARS
LAMBRETTA SCOOTERS
HONDA MOPED and MOTOR CYCLES
Mobylette — Raleigh — Capitano — Mopeds

WE STOCK ALL
LEADING MAKES OF CYCLES

IN JUNIOR SPORTS AND LIGHTWEIGHTS BY
**RALEIGH - SUN - HERCULES - CLAUD BUTLER
VIKING - DAWES - CARLTON - FALCON - ELSWICK
HOPPER - COVENTRY EAGLE - TRUSTY TRIUMPH**

We have the largest selection in South Yorkshire

H.P. TERMS   INSURANCE Etc.

Sales - Spares and Service

Always a large selection of new and used Motor Cycles,
Scooters, Cars and Vans in Stock.

ORDER NOW FOR CHRISTMAS

McDONALD'S
SWINTON ROAD - MEXBOROUGH

Tel. Mexborough 2377

See us on Stand 42 –44

WIGFALL'S
SPECIAL EXHIBITION OFFERS!

See COLOUR TELEVISION

FROM ONLY 27'6 WEEKLY RENTAL

Latest 19" Black and White T.V. FROM 7'6 Weekly Rental

FREE FOLD AWAY STEP STOOL
VALUE £5.21

HOOVER & PERSIL
RENT OR BUY A NEW
HOVER
AUTOMATIC OR TWIN TUB WASHER

PLUS UP TO £10 CASH DISCOUNT AND 38 WEEKS TO PAY

FREE GIFTS!
FOR THESE AND MANY OTHER EXCITING OFFERS — VISIT...

YOU CAN BE OUR QUEEN-OF-HEARTS AND WIN A FREE GIFT!

WIGFALL'S
EXHIBITION STAND
OR CALL IN AT
96 High Street, Mexborough

Above: Do you remember these old adverts?

Above: Main Street, looking towards West Street. The building on the right is the old Empress Ballroom, part of which is now Henry's Bar.

Below: Whittaker's Furnishers was located on the corner of Hartley Street and Main Street and became Pennine Motor Spares until its demolition in the 1980's. At this location now is a veterinary practice. The Belisha beacon and crossing no longer exist and the junction is controlled by a small round-about.

Above: Greens' butchers stood on the corner of High Street and Hope Street. This was later sold to Don Valley Sports and is now Intersport. The houses just below have now gone and the new Mexborough library has been built.

Below: Alexandre's was the gentlemens' outfitters directly opposite its rival Burton's menswear. It was closed in the 1970's when the whole row of shops was demolished to make way for the construction of the new precinct. The business never re-opened.

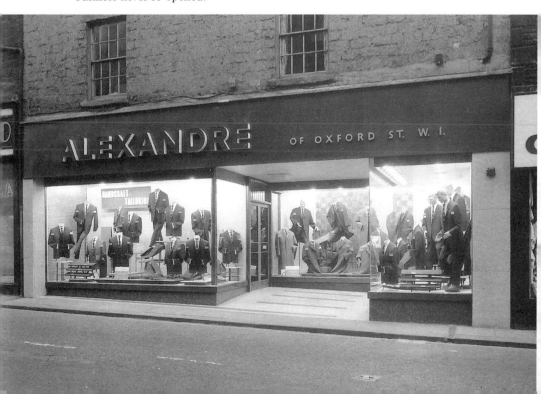

Above: A view of Church Street from Bank Street. In the background is the old Co-operative Bakery.

Below: This photograph shows High Street from Post Office Square showing The Wishing Well and Young's jewellers. Look at the car on the left of this picture, it is waiting for the traffic lights to change, at a once busy junction. There is no need for lights now as all traffic has been re-routed and this area is pedestrianized.

HAIR-DO

"Is it the usual again sir?"

I dropped the *Hornet* down a fraction and in the gloom of 'old man' Shirley's barber shop on the corner of Beaconsfield Street and Main Street, I watched Mr. Shirley, adjust his spectacles, and work his craft under a large but dully glowing overhead light. He was a tall thin man, with horn-rimmed glasses. Having very little hair, mainly consisting of a shiny, well plastered, black band of locks that ran around the sides and back of his head. The top, though equally shiny, was bald flesh. He always adorned a stiff collar and tie and a waistcoat beneath an off-white smock which was always left unbuttoned, swishing and flapping as he swaggered around his paying guests. The shop's interior was extremely gloomy with a colour scheme of wartime brown and cream. Everything about the premises was old, including Mr Shirley himself. But he was conveniently local and more importantly, so Dad said, he came highly recommended.

On this occasion I again watched him adjust his spectacles with the back of his hand and begin his styling on a gent whom I guessed was in his forties. The man was nodding awkwardly, indulging in light conversation as Mr Shirley held up long lengths of hair from the left hand side of the man's head and snipped at the ends.

There had been times when I'd turned out early for the barber's shop to find Mr Shirley in the throes of applying lather to the face of one of his customers. I had heard say that he gave the best cut-throat shave of anyone in the area. As I watched him whip the flashing blade of his open razor against a leather strap, fastened to a counter, and then test its sharpness by shaving hair off his forearm, I was extremely thankful I wasn't old enough to be in a position to practically judge that comment.

Leaning back on the black horsehair settle, that ran the width of the shop, my gaze returned to the pages of *The Hornet*, the football picture story strip 'The Ball of Fire' and was lost once more in the footer skills of Wally Brand. The monotonous conversation drifted into the background.

"Would you like something for the weekend sir?" Mr. Shirley asked mutely, and cleared his throat.

I dropped the comic onto my lap. Although I did not understand the significance of this address, I knew it signalled an end to this particular hair-cut, that was, whenever an adult sat in the big black leather looking chair. I mention this, because I had been caught out a few times, when he had not asked the same question whenever a young boy had sat in the chair, and it had resulted in Mr Shirley sloping across to me, demanding indignantly 'if it was my turn, and to stop day-dreaming.'

The barber put a final realigning parting, just above the left ear of his customer and swept it deftly over an almost bald pate, completing a style, something reminiscent of Bobby Charlton's.

The customer shook his head, smiled bleakly, and rose, dropping a handful of coins into the barber's outstretched hand.

I fingered the warm half-crown coin in my palm which Dad had reluctantly given me. As I was leaving the house I heard him chunter "two and six for a kid's haircut; that's flaming daylight robbery." And I had to agree as I thought what I could buy with it, instead.

Old man Shirley shook the plastic cape, giving off a sharp cracking noise with the whipping action, and then held it before me in a stance similar to a matador. "Your turn young man," he said and began pumping up the black chair, with his foot, by the use of a pedal at its base. As I leaned back, this chair for some strange reason reminded me of the dreaded dentist's, and I shuddered involuntarily.

"And what would we like?" he asked, combing his fingers through my shiny brown lanks.

In the mirror before me, which had several advertisement stickers around its edge, I looked at my hairstyle and then raised my eyes so I could meet 'old Shirley's' gaze.

"Can you change it to be a bit more modern?" I enquired.

He gave me a strange curious glance, that made me feel uncomfortable, then twisted my head from side to side. He huffed before curtly announcing, "Wouldn't suit you. There's nothing wrong with the style you've got. Look at that," he said, pointing to a 1950's Brylcreem poster to the side of the large mirror, which featured a shiny-haired man in a football pose. "That's Dennis Compton. Do you know who he is?"

I shook my head from side to side.

"Well Compton played football for Arsenal and England and cricket for Middlesex. He's a sporting hero and just look at his hairstyle. If it's good enough for him, then it's good enough for you."

He quickly reached into a cream coloured sterilizing cabinet on the wall, took out a fresh pair of scissors, and was snipping at my hair before I even thought of challenging his comment, and within five minutes Mr Shirley was greasing his palms with Brylcreem and dragging it through my shortened locks. A final flourish with hand and comb resulted in an unchanged style. Then with theatrical fashion he twirled a mirror several times in his hands and held it behind my head, nodding with approval. "There good as new," he proudly announced.

As I handed over the 2/6d, (two shillings and sixpence) to a vigorous rub down, from a brush, applied to the back of my neck, I had that uneasy feeling that I had just been quickly and professionally conned.

★ ★ ★ ★

Tony hovered in the background of my kitchen as I rubbed the smooth oily mixture into my palms and pushed vigorously at the few stubborn hairs that refused to stick in the crown of my head.

"Ar thought tha wor gonna get a Beatle-cut when tha went to Old Shirley's, the other day."

I watched him back through the wall mirror, where he was fingering the dowel shaft of my throwing arrow. Then I adjusted my head, where the crack was distorting the line of my parting. Satisfied, with a firm and final pat, that saw all resisting hairs in place, I turned sharply.

"Ar wor gonna, but he said I din't have the right type of hair for it." I lied.

"Is this thee new throwing arrow?" he asked, still rubbing his fingers up and down the wooden stick.

"Shush, keep thee voice down, me Mum dun't know I've got it. I med it secretly in the shed and I have to keep it hidden."

"Why?" he enquired dropping his voice.

"Well thar remembers when ar Glynis got hit in the face with one?"

Tony nodded.

"Well its ever since then. She says they're too dangerous and she med me throw mine away. I wun't have minded but ar weren't even there, when she got hit."

Tony shook his head and displayed a sympathetic gaze.

"Ar Glyn were reight lucky thar knows, 'fit an't been for her glasses stopping it, it'd had her eye out."

"Just like King Harold eh?" He giggled.

"Thar sick in't head," I exclaimed, then continued, "Does thar like me flights, I med 'em out of Jubilee carton, it gis 'em a fair old distance." I stroked the plastic coated fins slotted into the end of my throwing arrow.

"Has thar tried it out yet?"

"Just a practice. I chucked it reight ovver our house roof, and it landed on't outhouse. I reckon it'll go from one end of the footie pitch to the other."

Tony whistled between his teeth, "Let's go and have a go then."

I shouted upstairs, raising my voice above the scraping of wood on linoleum, where Mum was changing the furniture round in my bedroom, and then along with Tony, made our way to the park at the top of Schofield Street.

The park and fields had been recently cut and the perfume of freshly mown grass wafted into my nostrils. Mounds of loose cuttings were scattered throughout the confines of the field and several of my contemporaries were either throwing handfuls of grass or diving into the stacks. I considered joining one of the recognized groups, but then quickly dismissed the idea, as showing off my new throwing arrow was a more important event.

My two neighbours, Michael and Martin were playing cricket with some kids from round the corner. "Does thar want a game?" they called "One can go on each side."

I envied these two. They had a passion for cricket like I had for football, yet were far more adept. I had spent many an evening watching them in their back yard, bowling against chalked stumps on the outhouse, attracted by their regular calls of 'owzat.' They had tried to explain and show me how to deliver 'googlies', 'grasscutters', and 'spinners', but I continually and disappointingly frustrated their teachings, and they had given up on me, allowing me only to field instead. Subsequently I could not find an interest in the game and though I would have liked to play on this occasion I declined the offer, for fear of embarrassing myself in front of plenty of witnesses. I excused myself by informing them I had only come to try out my throwing arrow.

By the pavilion at the top of the field, several youths from the Highwoods estate were also in the process of showing off their own arrows, and one lad had even purchased a real archery arrow, with steel tip, which he had converted to throw by hand.

"Posh Get!" I whispered in Tony's ear, and he sniggered.

Wrapping the shoelace round two of my fingers and fitting a knotted end into the nick near the flight end, I pulled the lace tight, and lined up with the others, along the goalpost at one end of the pitch. With a short run I launched my arrow. It rose high and skimmed through the air beautifully, but fell short of my boasting, as it struck in the eighteen yard line of the opposite end.

"Ar thought thar said it would go ovver the pitch," sneered Tony.

"It wor only a practice. I wor just warming up," I replied defensively.

"Gis a go then. I bet ar can do it."

"No, thar can just wait now for saying that."

I could hear Tony grumbling as I strode along with the other arrow throwers to retrieve our missiles.

As I returned back to the base-line the sky overhead began to rumble, and grey clouds, which had suddenly appeared, loomed dark and ominous. Taking a step back to re-launch, the first spots of rain appeared. There was a loud crack overhead and within seconds the heavens had opened, and a deluge of rain hammered down. It was so hard and sharp that it stung. We all turned to head back for the pavilion, but I stopped in mid-stride as several mates looked on aghast, in my direction. A puzzled frown masked my face.

"What's up?" I exclaimed.

"Thee hairs foaming Mick," Tony replied.

Then I realized too late as the first suds trickled into my eyes. The pain was instantaneous and dancing coloured dots, which had entered my vision, became a forced blindness as I stumbled around. The pain was unbearable as I rubbed viciously at my closed eyelids.

In panic I dropped my new arrow and felt it snap beneath my footfall. It was hard to determine which was more painful – the loss of my new throwing arrow, or the continual stinging in my eyes.

"What's happened to thee hair?" Tony asked again.

I daren't reply as I turned in the direction of home. By now I was dripping wet and the pain continued unabated because I had to keep forcing open my eyes as I ran towards Schofield Street.

The last thing I dare tell anyone was that earlier that morning I couldn't find my usual Brylcreem and had decided to subordinate my hair using washing-up liquid!

A LIFE OF CRIME?

"Your Dad's got you a new bike."

At least that's what I thought Mum said as she removed a wooden peg from a row of them gripped firmly in her mouth, as she hung out the bed linen.

"What?" I requested. Wanting her to confirm what she had just muttered.

"Pardon, Michael, pardon. Not what."

Her lips never moved. The pegs never fell out. With a ventiloquist's dummy sitting on her lap she would have all the makings of a variety act.

"Pardon?" I reluctantly replied, knowing she would not repeat what she had initially announced unless I said the magic word. It did annoy me whenever Mum pulled me up over my occasionally wrong colloquialism. Especially in front of my mates. "Talk properly," she would always say. But I was talking properly. Only snobs, with plums in their gobs, talked eloquently. It was exactly the same whenever I uttered the word 'crap'. Mum would absolutely flip, threatening to wash my mouth out with soap. "Crap isn't swearing" I would coyly reply. Then she'd clip my ear, if I was in striking distance. "Don't say it again," she would demand.

"But it isn't swearing."

"It is. You know what it means Michael, so it's swearing."

Yet I never said the real word for the euphemistic term. At least not in Mum's presence. It was slang and all my mates used it. I put it down to the fact that Mum came from London, where all the posh people lived, and I guessed no one ever swore down there.

"Your Dad's managed to get you a second-hand bike," she continued, extracting another peg from her mouth, and clipped it on one of the thick grey woollen blankets. One could always tell summer had arrived when Mum removed and washed all the thick winter blankets from our beds.

"Great, when's it coming?"

Above: Where can you see dustbins like this any more? This picture shows the rear of the housing on Wilson Street. The row, that can be seen just through the snicket, is West Road.

"He's collecting it tonight after work.

I had struggled with my last bike for ages now. The seat and handlebars had been extended as far as they could go, yet still I was almost banging my knees on my chin whenever I peddled fast.

When I had spotted David from the top of the street with a new Chopper bicycle, I knew what I wanted. Bright red. it had three gears, with its own gear stick, just like my Uncle Horace's car. And when I had a 'backy' it was in comfort, because the seat was so long and it had a back rest. This really was a Rolls Royce amongst bikes. I had obviously mentioned this so many times that Dad had got a guilt complex and decided to buy me one. I could not wait for teatime.

From four o'clock onwards I must have run from the house to the bottom of Schofield Street a hundred times before I spotted Dad, in his work overalls; always splattered with pink dry plaster. I rushed beside him, dancing a warlike jig.

"Mam says you've got me a bike," I shouted jubilantly.

"It's second-hand Michael, but it's a beauty. It's been really well looked after. I'm picking it up after tea." he removed the khaki 'snap bag' from his shoulder and jogged forwards.

"Race you home," he said as I tried to complete two steps to his one stride.

* * * * *

Have you ever been to those dizzy heights, where all the excitement, wonderment and thrill absorbs every space of your body and then been brought quickly down to terra-firma with such earth-shattering anti-climax? Well for half-an-hour that summer's day that's how I felt when I saw Dad wheeling my new bicycle towards me down the passage.

"Well what do you think? It's in really good nick ain't it?"

I desperately tried not to look let down as the image of a bright red Chopper disappeared and fading in came this dark green wartime bike, with it's sit-up-and-beg handlebars and metal calliper brakes. Back in the late 1940's I'm sure any young boy would have given his eyeteeth for such a wonderful cycle, but in the 1970's kids like me had to be 'with it' and 'groovy'.

However this unappreciative streak disappeared within half an

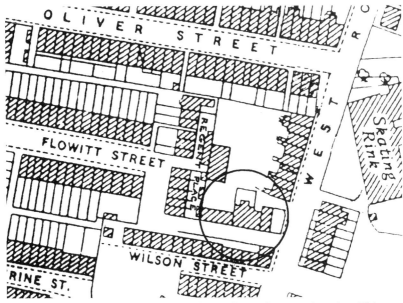

Above: The ringed area on the map, inset, shows the exact location. This row of houses together with Regent Place and Wilson Street were all demolished to make way for the construction of Blenheim Crescent flats.

Below: This row of houses is part of Regent Place, which was at the top, and faced onto, Flowitt Street. Through the snicket, at the front of this picture, led into a small paddock where some horses used to graze. Locals knew this area as *'Big Yard.'*

Above: This row of houses backed onto *'Big Yard'* and was attached to *'Mineral House'* (still exists).

hour, as I got my head around the fact that Dad could not actually afford a Chopper, and this was the best his money could buy. This was also compounded by the acceptance of it from my friends, as they all asked 'for a try,' and then commented on how smooth it was to ride. By the end of the evening my spirits had risen, especially as it easily moved ahead of David's Chopper, as we raced around the block.

★ ★ ★ ★ ★

Within weeks, because I was efficiently mobile, I had secured myself a paper round.

This was not only a wonderful opportunity to earn more spending money, but it also gave me access to a whole host of reading material, as I dallied on my route, with various comics balanced across my handlebars which I managed to read before posting them at their destination. Because of this, on more than one occasion, I had close scrapes with doddering pedestrians, who seemed to suddenly appear, whilst I had become unawaringly engrossed in the exploits of characters from COR, WHIZZER & CHIPS; an old favourite, THE WIZARD; and most recently THE MARVEL, in which every known super-hero is crammed into one comic.

I'd begun my paper round, at the newsagents owned by Mr Severns, on Main Street, in the springtime, and within weeks knew every short cut on the route, soon enabling me to knock many minutes off my completion time. during the summer

Right: The Spider-Man comic followed on the back of the successful Marvel. These first three issues also show the free gift of Super-hero stickers, which came with the third edition.

months I was amazed at just how quiet the streets could be at 6.30am, and it gave me every opportunity to race down Barber's Path and pull a skid on Gorney's park.

However as the days got shorter and the mornings darker and colder, I became less enthusiastic about jumping out of a warm bed. Realistically though I still managed to get a 'dab' on', as I peddled like fury, so that I could get back to a blazing coal fire and a steaming cup of tea.

The money I earned, gave me wealth I had never previously appreciated, and for the first time I was in a position to develop a savings account. Though I soon discovered, as the winter months dragged on, that I had to continually dip into my cash to replace the batteries in my rear lamp. I was very fortunate that the front light worked off a dynamo, because I was soon having to purchase two lots of batteries every week. And with no tax exemptions replenishing my back lamp was soon becoming a very expensive commodity. With this in mind I soon found myself juggling with the thought of either breaking the law, by not displaying a back light, or using up all my hard earned cash on batteries. It was no contest. The sound of jingling currency was far more important than the laws of the land.

Although frosty and cold, it was extremely clear the first day that my batteries had run down, and so leaving my back lamp on the kitchen table I peddled like Billy-Oh in the direction of Severns newsagents. I can recall thinking what a stupid law it was when the street lighting was perfectly adequate to allow others to see me on my bike.

I had just passed Marjories' hairdressers on Main Street when I noticed him, lurking in the doorway shadows of David Haigh's small hardware store, by the corner of Belmont Street. Terror froze my limbs rigid as I saw the black cape waft in the early morning breeze. A cold tingling shiver traced itself all the way up my spine, lifting the hairs on my neck – and it wasn't the winter chill to blame. I tried to brake carefully, but the metal calliper system shrieked loudly. My nerveless hands lost their grip, as I wobbled for a second, whilst trying to spin the bike around. Then the sturdy upright figure stepped into the open, silver crest of the police badge, shimmering on the black

Above: This aerial photograph takes you (bottom left) from Post Office Square, out right into the town centre. You then travel up towards Garden Street. Take notice of the large house on that street and the back-to-backs on Sarah and Charles Streets (at the rear of the Post Office). These have now been demolished and the cleared area is car parking space.

The new buildings under construction, (left-centre) are the dormer-bungalows now near the junction of Garden Street and Dolcliffe Road. Top left is the area I knew locally as 'Gorneys', where there was a small park and a steep face of limestone rock, from which one could find an abundance of fossils. This land was actually owned by my Great Grandfather and given to Mexborough Urban District Council, to be developed into the park, when he was Chairman. Then travelling up and along Dolcliffe Road, just going right out of the photograph is the stone building, where I used to play and 'nest'. That building was Albert Terrace. The majority of the buildings in this photo have now been demolished.

background of the tall helmet.

Absolute fear encased my whole body. I could not believe my bad luck. The first time I had made a deliberate conscious decision to break the law and a Policeman was lying in wait.

My brain was working overtime, as in a split-second I was

deciding what to do. I thought quickly. Here I am on my bike and there's nearly two hundred yards between us. I can easily outrun him. I flicked the pedal up and slammed my right foot down hard. Every ounce from my skinny limbs was forced into ramming those pedals around.

My form was bent low over the frame of my bulky bike, as I sprinted towards Schofield Street, well out of reach from the long arm of the law. I peddled furiously round the corner of the street, head down, legs pistoning, the bicycle lying at a perilous angle as I swept round. Then I was up again. For a second I was Donald Campbell going for the world speed record, until I remembered what had happened to him, and I shrugged it from my brain.

I made it home in no time and just before I threw my bike into the passage I glanced down the road. There was no sign of the officer, only a couple of miners, on the corner of Brittain Street, waiting to be picked up for their shift.

Breathing sharply, trying to contain the panic that had welled up inside me, I fastened the now retrieved bike lamp to the rear of the cycle, tapping it sharply to encourage a dull glow to emit.

Now if I went back along Catherine Street and dropped down through Simpson's Place, I thought smiling, I should easily avoid the searching Bobby.

I had just managed to clip the flat metal fastener in place when the deep gruff tone startled me. 'WHAT DO YOU THINK YOU'RE DOING?'

I first clapped sight on a shiny pair of boots and my heart was beating wildly as my gaze shot up to meet the Constable's probing eyes.

My expression changed with startling sharpness. A kind of terror flickered in my eyes and sweat rolled down from my armpits, tickling my ribs, underneath a bri-nylon shirt. Caught red-handed, and I began to stammer.

'Well, what are you up to young man?'

I feared the worst. Clapped in irons for deliberately flouting the law. The scenes from Z-Cars were suddenly becoming reality. 'I forgot, I forgot my back light,' I stammered.

'Is it your bike?'

His investigative voice was unnerving me. I not only shook uneasily, I positively trembled with fear. 'Yes. My Dad bought it for me,' I managed to quake.

'What are you playing at then eh?'

This was becoming an uncomfortable line of serious questioning. 'I'm just going on my paper round.'

'Why did you run away then?'

'When I saw you, I just remembered I'd forgot my back light.'

'So you were riding without lights hey?' He hooked fingers of both hands beneath the buttons of his two top pockets and began shaking his head from side to side. My teeth clenched tight. I never blinked and I was sure my eyes would burst from their sockets. 'I'd forgotten them sir.'

He tutted for a moment. 'Well young man. I'm going to let you off with a warning on this occasion. But I'll be watching you very carefully from now on.' His face twisted in composure to a sterner glare and he held up a warning hand, from out of one tunic pocket, balancing on the balls of his feet. 'I never forget a face, so be warned. If I ever catch you riding without lights again it'll be the high jump for you. do you understand?'

'Yes, yes sir.' My whole skeleton had now turned to jelly. I felt weak at the knees and the pit of my stomach was empty.

Having delivered his warning judicially he turned smartly and I could have sworn he had a wry smile as he plodded away. At that moment, on reflection, I wasn't surprised I had been caught out, because there was hardly a sound from his soft-soled boots.

As I plucked up courage to continue my paper round I thought long and hard as to how he had known where I'd gone. I put it down to the training they receive in the powers of detection. I must have left some tell-tale signs allowing him to trace my steps to home. No wonder the great train robbers had been caught.

For nights afterwards I had a vivid dream about our back door being kicked in to shouts of 'open up in the name of the law.'

★ ★ ★ ★ ★

Every morning on my way to school I would invariably take

the same route, which was along Dolcliffe Road and then cut through the houses and up onto waste land. Here there was a large imposing substantial stone building, which I originally thought because of its design was a mansion, yet later learned was a small row of houses called Albert Terrace. I can never recall them in use and unfortunately the buildings had become dilapidated, with their final remaining occupants being starlings and swifts. These fine old houses and outbuildings became a marvellous arena for an abundance of games within the ruined confines. The front looked down on an enclosed lawn, and someone did mention to me once that this was once the Terraces tennis courts. Sadly those gardens had become a wilderness. In fact there was an air of complete desolation about the place. Once beautiful trees now stood amongst a tangle of bramble and weeds; but what a marvellous haunt to go nesting.

Below: Adwick Road Junior School. A school I so fondly remember, where I forged many early friendships and where I also seemed prone to numerous accidents which required hospital treatment. Yet it was also a breeding ground for a whole host of juvenile escapism. Recollections of imaginative games, duplicating heroes from television programmes. There was Batman; The Champions; Land of the Giants; Man from UNCLE, and Mission Impossible, to name but a few. Then there was the game of 'Finger, thumb, a little dumb, a little granny,' marbles, and collectors' card games, with our swaps, against the wall of the boys' toilet. 'Tiggy' and the more daring 'Kiss Catch' was at the opposite end of the playground, behind the rear of Class 8 and the girls' toilets.

This school no longer exists, having been demolished in the 1980's. The tall building to the left was the woodwork section of the Secondary school, on College Road. This has also been demolished.

This became a regular route which then took me across Carlisle Street and onto a disused park which bordered on the old Dolcliffe Road school. The last part of my journey prior to reaching school was squeezing between a row of corrugated garages on Cromwell Road and through the backings into College Road.

One morning I was making this familiar trek and just as I had tramped onto the disused park, opposite the Hope Club, I saw a group of local kids milling around in an unorganized huddle. My immediate thought was 'scrap,' but as I put on a spurt of speed and drew nearer, the usual cries, barracking and caterwalls, one associates with schoolboy displays of fisticuffs, was not to be heard, and the mystery intensified.

It was necessary to jostle amongst them in order to discover just what the hue and cry was about.

In two large cardboard boxes, one of which had the black bold letters of OMO printed across its exterior, I saw a magnificent haul of all manner and types of confectionery. There were disturbed cartons of Black Jacks, Fruit Salads, Sherbert Dips and Lucky Bags scattered inside the huge boxes. A whole group of kids were ferreting amongst the novelties, extracting as many items as they could muster before traipsing away in smaller clusters.

'Whose is all this?' I enquired to no one in particular, having replaced a space vacated by one of the youths and now my own hands were picking out a selection of sweets.

'Dun't know,' someone answered. 'Everyone's getting some spice.'

I paused, only momentarily. 'They're not here as a trap are they? Poisoned like?'

A few faces looked towards me, their own digits suddenly frozen amongst the confectionery

Then one remarked, 'Naw, some of me mates have been scoffing them early doors and their all reight.' He bundled a handful of packets into his blazer pockets.

After rummaging for a few more seconds I pulled out two packets of Opal fruits, a fistful of Black Jacks and a whole host of different liquorice novelties. I then left with several other individuals, each of us examining our parcels and commenting about the free windfall.

There was a brief exchange of views and furrowed brows in an attempt to determine how the sweets had been left there. But with the best suggestion being: 'Must be local election time; me Dad sez Councillors are allas bribing people, this must be summat new. We dismissed it and merely hoped it would be a regular event.

Even with a slow meander we were still allowed ample time in the cloakrooms to boast and display our array of free sweets to the less fortunate. Close friends were allowed a few samples and I proudly strutted like a cock-hen, chewing exaggeratedly, until I felt a slap on my shoulder. It caught me by surprise and I almost swallowed the mouthful of Black Jack, making me wince as I spun around.

Tony was red and flushed and gasping for breath. 'Mick, has thar been on't fields near't Hope Club this morning?'

I dislodged the chewy sweet from the back of my throat and rolled it to the front of my mouth.

'Yar stupid pillock. What's thy hit me like that for? Thar nearly med me choke to death.'

He glanced at the two packets of Opal Fruits firmly clenched in my hands, 'Thy ain' got them from't fields as thar?'

'What if I have?' I replied puzzled.

'Cos cops are all ovver place. Somebody brok into a spice shop last neet and dumped the stuff behind an 'edge. Fuzz are talking to loads of kids who've had some of 'em.'

A wave of panic rose up from some dark place and engulfed me, the sense of impending disaster crushing down upon me. I took a deep breath and held it for a moment, and as the blind panic receded I felt weak and shaken. 'I din't know they were nicked. What's thar think'll happen?'

'Probably everyone'll get arrested when they come to school.'

With mouth wide open I was gasping for air, my throat burning and dry. 'Oh God, I feel awful. Me Dad'll kill me.'

'Thy'll end up in court wie a record.'

I shook my head with fumbling uncertainty, like someone waking up out of their worst nightmare. 'Shut thee gob Tony.'

Just then I saw Martin hanging up his parka and an idea cascaded inside my head. 'Hey-op Martin.'

He turned sharply. A face that always looked like it was splattered with brown paint, such was the abundance of freckles, shot a glance in my direction.

'Are these thy Opal Fruits?' I said, holding out my hand and showing him the two yellow packets.

He glanced nervously, unsure, from my face to hands, 'Why?'

'Cos I've just found 'em on't cloakroom floor. I thought thar might have dropped 'em out of thee coat.'

He hesitated, his eyes now darting all over the place. Looking at his green fur-hooded parka, then at me, and finally Tony.

Our faces were dead-pan.

'Er, yeah, yeah. Thanks for finding them.' He almost snatched them out of my hand. As he exited quickly I nudged Tony sharply in the ribs.

'There's one born every minute,' I said with great relief.

There were a lot of dreary faces that morning at break-time. I recognized many as those who had been with me, pilfering the sweets from the boxes in the fields. Amongst them I spotted Martin skulking near the boys' toilets. I sidled up to him.

'Hey-op, what's up, thar looks miserable?'

He looked up at me with a face that looked as though he wanted my blood. It was a good job he couldn't fight.

'Did thar really find them spice on the floor?' he stammered out impatiently.

'Course ar did. Why? Thar sed they were thine.' I replied poker-faced.

'Cos I've just got reight done.'

'What for?' I continued the charade.

'The cops have been in't school this morning about some break-in at a spice shop and somebody gave my name cos they saw me with those Opal Fruits.'

'Weren't they thine then?'

'Course not. Ar wor lying to thee just to get some free spice. Well it got me done din't it. I tried to tell 'em they were nowt to do wie me but I dunt think they believed 'me.'

'N-E-V-E-R.'

'Ar, there were a reight load of us in't headmaster's office. We had a reight bollockin'. Ar were fair crappin' mesen.'

'Thar din't tell 'em who thar got 'em off, did thar?'

'Naew, course not. Anyroad they never let us say ought. Just kept sharting and rawping at us.' He paused. ''Ave been throwin' up in't bogs all mornin' thar knows.'

'Well ar'll tell thee what. Ar'll gie thee some of me footy card swaps for not grassing on me. Is that all reight?'

His face lightened up. 'That'll be great, but thar dun't need to, that knows. Ar know it want thy fault.'

* * * * *

Above: Mexborough Town F.C. was founded in 1962 and entered the Yorkshire League, Division 2. In their first season they became runners-up and promoted to Division 1, where again, in the 1963-64 season they were runners-up as well as County Cup Finalists.

My interest in football began at the Athletic ground, when my Grandad, who was President of the club, introduced me as programme seller and ball-boy. Sadly the club began to decline in the early 1970's as fans drifted away, having easier access to cars which allowed them to watch more prominent Football league clubs.

Mexborough Town FC finally succumbed to financial pressure in the early 1980's, and folded.

W. CROWCROFT
AND SONS LIMITED
Mexborough.
WHOLESALE FRUITERERS
&
POTATO MERCHANTS
Tel. Mex. 2107   Established over 70 years

Call at
THE CONCERTINA
CLUB
for a Good Drink
Before The Match
50 yds. from the Ground

Mexboro' Town
Football Club
SUPPORTERS
CLUB

Headquarters:
Montague Arms Hotel,
High Street,   Mexborough.
Tel: 3185

MEMBERSHIP
CARD

Wilf Oakley, Printer, Swinton

Mexborough Town
Football Club

Mexboro' Athletic Ground
HAMPDEN ROAD, MEXBRO'

Season Ticket

Adults 15/-

Main Street, Mexboro'

Mexborough Town
Football Club

Mexboro' Athletic Ground
HAMPDEN ROAD, MEXBRO'

Season Ticket
1964-1965

Childrens Price
O. A. P.   5/-
Ladies

R. Bannister, Mexborough

MEXBOROUGH TOWN
FIXTURES 1964-65

1964

Aug.	22—Bridlington Trinity	.....	H
	29—Harrogate Town	....	H
Sept.	5—Hatfield Main	....	H
	12—Farsley Celtic	....	A
	19—Hull Brunswich	....	H
	26—Ossett Albion	....	A
Oct.	3—Wombwell S.A.	....	H
	10—Scarborough	....	A
	17—Bridlington Town	....	H
	24—Harrogate Railway	....	A
	31—Swillington	....	H
Nov.	7—Yorkshire League Cup		
	14—Rawmarsh	....	H
	21—Hallam	....	A
	28—Hallam	....	H
Dec.	5—County Cup		
	12—Yorkshire League Cup		
	19—Harrogate Town	....	A

	Wombwell S.A.	....	A
	—Scarborough	....	H
	—County Cup		
	20—Harrogate Railway	....	H
	27—Swillington	....	A
Mar.	6—Selby Town	....	H
	13—Rawmarsh	....	A
	20—Bridlington Town	....	A
	27—Brodsworth	....	A
Apr.	3—Bridlington Trinity	....	H
	10—Selby Town	....	A
	17—Hull Brunswich	....	A
	24—		

"Subject to alteration for "F.A." Cup."

Above: Mexborough Athletic ground was once a hive of activity not only when Mexborough Town played there but also when the summer months brought regular cricket matches to the club's ground.

Stewart was one of those friends that you suddenly bump into and realize you have a lot in common with. That commonality was football.

He knew all the famous players; had a bedroom full of SHOOT magazines, from which he shared all manner of tactics, – from the professionals - no less; and he was also in the process of collecting the World Cup coin series of the England team, like myself. He lived in a terraced house that was infinitely larger than ours and there was enough room in his bedroom to actually play with his Scalextric race circuit.

In the summer months I had taken to calling on him regularly whilst on the way to school. It was somewhat earlier than normal, because it gave us time to go via West Street park, where he could show me some of the ball skills he had learned from his football magazines.

I liked to discuss Mexborough Town, where I was a ball-boy and programme seller. Gushing over the fact that their newest striker had come from a fouth division side, and I'd been to his house and actually held this professional footballer's grass-snake. The first few times I mentioned this, Stewart was in awe. However as I continued to repeat myself he simply told me to

Above: This aerial photograph takes you from Garden Street and into the top end of High Street. The majority of this property has now been demolished and a new town centre development is in place. To the left one can see an open piece of land. When Market Street was being demolished for the new bypass, the market stalls were transferred to this site and an open market operated here for several years before its relocation to its present site, in the centre of High Street.

As you travel above centre and right of the picture, just in front of the canal, is Holmes' Pop factory and West Street park. The present bypass now runs left to right almost through the centre of this photograph.

Top right is the Mexborough Locomotive sheds. These no longer exist.

'shut me gob' and so the name-dropping came to an end.

One morning we were just leaving his house as normal when he picked up his shiny brown case football, by its loose lace, and swung it towards me. I rose to meet it with my head, but instead of it bouncing away, the soft leather buffeted my skull, denting its circumference. A surging whoosh of rushing air exploded from the unlaced gap and Stewart started to laugh.

'It's bust,' I said with disgust, kicking the mishaped casey towards him.

When we got to the park he made several attempts to show me how many times he 'could keep it up' but with a bust case-ball it was a cumbersome ordeal that failed repeatedly. Stewart snatched it furiously from the ground, swinging it wildly with its lace and then booted it with such ferocity that it shot over the perimeter fence into Holmes' pop yard. 'Come on we'll tek a short cut,' he said, and with a spring in his step, he bolted towards the concrete fence.

At this stage I developed a sense of trepidation even though I was sprinting after him. I felt uncomfortable with trespassing into the pop yard. 'We can't go in theer, we'll get done if we get caught.'

'Will we eckers. I allas tek a short cut through theer. Thee leave it to me, it'll be reight.'

I was still apprehensive as we vaulted a broken down section of the concrete fencing that boundaried onto Holmes's.

As I dropped into the yard I was awe-struck by the amount of pallet-stacks, which seemed to stretch as far as the eye could see, of full, as well as empty pop bottles.

'Come on I'll show thee summat,' Stewart hissed in a low tone. 'Keep thee noise down.'

Now I really was unsure as I watched his stooped frame flit fleetingly from one stack to the other like a soldier trained in urban guerrilla tactics. As I followed, it was extremely unnerving and my ears and eyes were strained to their limits as I recognized adult voices close by, as well as the thumping of engines from fork lift trucks.

Stewart had already retrieved his ball as we suddenly reached a stack of wooden pallets. These were piled to excess with boxes each emblazoned with the logo of X-L crisps.

'Just keep thee eyes peeled,' he whispered.

Stewart glanced quickly around and then punched a clenched fist through the side of one of the boxes. My heart thrashed against chest walls as several red and blue packets of crisps spewed out of the gap. He grabbed a handful and forced them into the open lace-flap of his busted casey. I looked on horrified. By now I could actually hear my heart pounding as I feared it would burst through my rib cage.

He selected a few more packets of plain crisps, bundled them inside the ball, patted it into a more rounded shape and then swiftly fastened the laces tight.

A sudden emptiness swamped me as he smiled in my direction.

'Reight let's get out of here.'

He must have recognized the terror masking my face. 'Dunt worry, I do it regular.'

We had just turned to go back to the fencing; I personally could not wait to get away; when a voice boomed in our direction.

'OY WHAT ARE YOU TWO DOING?'

Above: This view of the bypass was taken shortly after its opening. To the left hand side one can still see what was left of the streets of West, Shelley, Hope, Glasshouse Lane and Market Street. These were later demolished in the late 1970's and the new Shopping complex and indoor market built. This area now also has the bus station.

My head whipped round in stunned disbelief. I was speechless. My whole life flashing before my eyes.

Stewart hesitated for only a fraction. 'We've just come to get our ball back mister.' Then he launched it in the air, met it with his forehead and directed it neatly towards me. There was a strange rustle and I don't know how; it must have been instinctive; but I actually caught it.

'WELL YOU SHOULDN'T BE IN HERE' the man continued shouting, 'YOU'RE TRESPASSING. NOW

Below: In the bottom shot, to the right, one can just see some of the stalls of the re-located outside market, and to the left the factory units of Modern Methods.

BUGGER OFF AND DON'T COME BACK.'

I didn't need any further warning as I shot towards the concrete fence. I somehow managed to clear it, even though I was still clutching the ball.

Back inside West Street park I paused for a few seconds to settle and regulate my breathing and Stewart snatched back the ball.

'What did you do that for?' I gasped 'I could have died when you headed the ball to me.'

He started to laugh raucously 'Well nar thar can't say owt, can thar. Cos thar just as guilty. If thar snitches thy'll get done for handling nicked goods. - By the way, does thar want a bag o' crisps?'

Needless to say I didn't accept, and I kept my distance from Stewart after that, containing my friendship to kick abouts in the school yard.

For a few seconds, whilst inside Holmes's pop yard that day, I realized I could never handle a life of crime. Continuously looking over one's shoulder for fear of a Constable sneaking up on you is an extremely unpleasant feeling. Now I realize what Ronnie Biggs must have gone through.

Below: The large roundabout has been drastically reduced for the increased flow of traffic.

Above: Madame Florence's classic fashions began on High Street and stayed well into the 1970's before being demolished as part of the new town centre layout. The fashion shop has since expanded and now occupies two units in Montagu Chambers.

Below: Fred Ward's wholesale warehouse stood on Market Street when he had his shop on High Street. This was demolished when the by pass was built and the wall to the right is now part of the flyover. Public toilets now stand at this location.
Fred Ward's shop has changed hands but a stall run by his family is at the new outdoor market.

Above: These factory units of Modern Methods were on Cliffe Street. In their day they were a large employer of local people. In the 1980's these units were demolished when the business closed and in its place there are now several industrial units housing a variety of business firms.

Below: These original shops were situated on Bank Street by Dolcliffe Road and were demolished because of subsidence. They have since been rebuilt in their original stone and style.

CIDER, WOMEN AND SONG

"Hey-op, where's thar going." Turning sharply to my left and looking back along Wood Street I saw Danny and David kicking a leather casey against the framework of David Haigh's closed entrance gate. I had known and associated with these two brothers for as long as I could remember and they shared the same passion for football as myself. They were part of the Wood Street clan who regularly challenged Schofield Street Rovers. We always managed to beat them, though to hear them reminisce I sometimes felt that I had played in a different game. To listen to them, it was nearly always a draw, or they had been robbed in the dying minutes. However, whatever the outcome - dubious or otherwise - friendship between us always remained the 'status quo'.

"It's Friday, the Empress disco is open," I called back stepping towards them, but then halted as I realized that if I got embroiled in a game of one-kick with them, it would inevitably mean the spoiling of my new cream 'sta-press' and the scuffing of freshly polished brogues.

"Disco," Danny huffed "Thats for poofs."

"Nay it ain't, all me mates go."

"They're poofs as well," He indignantly recalled, swiftly kicking the brown casey against the crimson wooden panels, rattling the padlocked gate.

"Hey does thar like my new shirt? Its a Ben Sherman thar knows," I said attempting to change the subject whilst tugging at the collar of my red and white checked shirt. "Looks like me Gran's tablecloth," came back a sniggering retort.

"Thar only jealous; any road I'm seeing this lass toneet, she's a reight dancer, showed me how to do the 'Woolly Bully', bet thar can't do that."

"Thar seeing a lass" Danny continued to ridicule, "Thy'll be telling us thar packing in footy next, ya poof."

"Ar wain't and any road it's moor fun than playing with thee."

As I strode away the sound of leather against wood was diminishing by the second.

★ ★ ★ ★ ★

I recognized many faces amongst the throng of young people who milled around Swinton Road, waiting to go inside The Empress ballrooms which had recently opened on Friday evening for a teenages disco. I was beginning to take notice of things happening around me. Recently I had been introduced to the taste of music and had tended towards the sounds of T.Rex and David Bowie whilst my fashion sense leant towards 'Mods; with a particular distaste towards 'Rockers' and 'Greasers'. There were also girls now looming on the horizon and on that subject I preferred to keep my options open for the time being.

"We're going for some moor cider, ar thar coming Mick?" Billy gave me a sharp nudge. He was just one of the new characters that I had recently become associated with, which previously I had hardly acknowledged. The new association was our common taste in music and clothes. However there was one amongst the crowd that I had become nervous around and I was pretty sure I wasn't the only one. That was Dave. He was a complete braggart. He'd done everything. He'd fought everyone. He talked of committing crime as though he was one of the Kray twins. He particularly disturbed me when he started acting stupidly after sniffing Lady Esquires shoe polish splashed onto a handkerchief. It was Dave who had introduced me to Cider and he was the one with the courage to buy it from the off-licence. It was my first introduction to illegal alcohol and I liked the added 'buzz' it gave me to 'chat up the lasses,' something which previously had always left me red faced and tongue-tied.

The full bottle of cider, which Dave had got for me and the half I had gulped from Billy's second bottle had given me a real spring in my step and I had to forcibly hold my breath as I passed the 'bouncer' on the Empress door.

The inside of the place was teeming with teenagers like myself.

In the dance hall, to my right, there was row upon row of dancing girls, dressed in checked or tartan 'Chelsea bags' with similarly coloured scarves tied around their wrists, bopping to the music of the Bay City Rollers.

I scoured my eyes around the dim interior hoping to gain sight

Below: This 1960's photograph shows the newly refurbished bar inside the Empress ballroom. The club boasted that it had one of the finest dance floors in the north.

of the girl who had taught me the steps of 'Woolly Bully', but unfortunately the activity in the room interrupted my gaze.

It was at this stage the warm glow feeling had disappeared and was being replaced by a strange queasy sensation. I wasn't sure if it was the flashing lights because my head was suddenly swirling and my stomach fluttering. I quickly decided I needed the toilet.

Very quickly.

Scampering downstairs, past the cloakroom, I just made it in time as I flung myself at the toilet bowl.

The first belch burnt the back of my throat, the second brought up a whoosh of watery vomit and the third a wave of bile, which again burnt my throat. I belched and gipped several more times before recovering to dab at the sweat that was leaking from my brow.

The next five minutes was spent washing my face and slapping my cheeks, in front of the mirror, in an attempt to rid them of their paleness so that I could venture back upstairs. I was totally embarrassed by my predicament, doubtless brought on by my cocky over-indulgence of cider.

I hoped the forced smile I bore would cover the uncomfortable feeling I still had as I put on a burst of energy as an attempt to show there was nothing wrong with me. At the entranceway to the dance hall I spotted her. That graceful movement from the girl who had taught me to dance. I just had to talk to her whilst I still had the 'Dutch courage.' Enthusiastically I sidled up to her and as I approached she had her back to me. I guessed I must have tapped her shoulder too fiercely judging by the scowling reception she gave me. Composing myself swiftly I said "Remember me?"

"Oh yes." That voice of hers was so soft. Almost angelic.

"I've remembered thar knows."

"What?" She seemed puzzled.

I kicked out my legs. "Woolly Bully. What thar taught me."

"Oh, right." She was still dancing whilst she talked and my head swayed with her gyrating hips. It was at this time I became aware that some of the girls around her were sniggering. Though I was determined they wouldn't distract me from 'chatting her up' as I gazed at those gleaming white teeth beneath her soft lips. "Do you wanna dance now?"

"I'm with my mates."

"Well thar can still dance wie me as well."

"No not whilst I'm with my mates I can't."

"Go on just one." I pushed myself forwards, remembering what my friends had told me, about how all girls liked their men to be masterful. These were friends with previous experience with girls and if they were giving me wise words, then I must put them into action. She was bound to respond if I was positive. "Come on I'm only asking for one dance."

I loomed closer.

"I said NO."

"Oh go on, just once."

"No. Now push off and don't come back, thar smells of spew."

The sniggering from the girls around me became laughter and a sudden red flush engulfed the waxness of my face. My first youthful encounter with girls had proved a complete disaster.

Above: This photograph of the canal at Ferryboat Lane, was taken in the late 1950's, when only a swing bridge allowed access over the canal, with the remainder of the journey to Old Denaby being completed by ferry boat across the River Don.

Below: In 1963 a concrete and metal foot bridge was erected to span both the canal and the river. The original swing bridge was still in place when this photograph was taken.

These last photographs were taken in the late 50's by the borough surveyor of Mexborough Urban District Council prior to the area being demolished in the 1960's. As yet I have been unable to identify the exact location of these photographs. The same children appear in both photographs and the eldest boy will now be in his 50's. Do you recognise him or the area?

ACKNOWLEDGEMENTS

My special thanks go out to the following who contributed photographs which assisted me in completing this book:

Giles Brearley for his father's photographs, depicting many streets in Mexborough taken for the Urban Council, prior to their demolition.

To Paul Walters for the use of part of his father's vast collection (Walters Studios of Mexborough).

Also, once again to Gary Barker and The Mexborough Heritage Society; and finally to Graham Walker for the use of his memorabilia throughout this book.